Queen

Lessons from Esther

Julia A. Royston

Edited by: Claude R. Royston

BK Royston Publishing
Jeffersonville, IN

BK Royston Publishing
P. O. Box 4321
Jeffersonville, IN 47131
502-802-5385
http://www.bkroystonpublishing.com
bkroystonpublishing@gmail.com

Cover Design: Brent Barnett

ISBN-13: 978-1-946111-66-1

Printed in the United States of America

Dedication

To every woman who has ever been
treated less than a Queen.

Acknowledgements

First, I acknowledge my Lord and Savior Jesus Christ for giving me all of my gifts and especially my gift to write His words.

My husband who is always supportive, loving and encouraging me to utilize all of my gifts and talents. Thank you honey.

To my mother, Dr. Daisy Foree, who is my number one cheerleader and always tells me, "hang in there, you can do it." To my father, Dr. Jack Foree, who is never far away from me in spirit or my heart. I only have to look in the mirror each day to see him.

To Rev. Claude and Mrs. Lillie Royston who support me in everything I do. Especially, Rev. Royston for his careful eye to detail and his sensitive heart to content.

To the rest of my family, I love you and thank you for your prayers, support and love.

Table of Contents

Introduction

Today I hear the term Queen and/or King used quite frequently. The movie Black Panther helped escalate this use of the term on the street after so many around the world saw the depiction of African royalty on the big screen. I enjoyed the movie very much. I also watched intently the British Royal Wedding of Prince Harry to Meghan Markle with enthusiasm and excitement. The pomp and circumstance throughout the ceremony and the broadcasts were incredible. This very popular and well-known young woman was saying no to Hollywood and now saying, yes to a Prince was every young girl's dream. All girls are princesses awaiting prince, right? Because I don't live in a monarchy ruled country, I really needed the narrators and facilitators to inform and explain so many things, introduce and distinguish the people and their titles that were the invited guests and participants throughout the wedding ceremony. Their comments were priceless. All of the rules, regulations and traditions that had to be followed was overwhelming to hear about let alone know that now, this very American young woman's life was be changed forever after marrying this prince. She would now be guided and subjected to a whole new life with little or no pre-requisites just a descent upbringing, love in her heart and a yes. Oh, how much that yes would entail.

I recently was asked to speak at a women's tea on the Esther Anointing. The Tea was initially postponed and when I thought I was off the hook from speaking and delivering what God gave me, he said, "write the book of what I gave you." So here we go...

God let me know throughout my study that He is going to soon gather, "His Bride" but He too, like King Ahasuerus is looking for a replacement for royalty on earth. He needs a Queen, a bride who is exemplifying his attributes and characteristics on earth as "it is in heaven." Queen Vashti refused the requests of the King Ah As a modern woman, reading the Book of Esther and all that took place at the banquet and then realizing the King's request is somewhat debatable as to whether I would have performed my "Queen" duties considering they had been intoxicated for days. What a sight? But it was the King that was making the request and she said, no. It sent the other dignitaries and officers into an uproar. "What if other women refused to obey the requests of their husbands in leadership?" The downfall of the Kingdom was sure to ensue. From Esther 1, this was the predicament that the Persian kingdom found itself in, a non-compliant Queen, disobeying the King. We serve the King of Kings. He made clear to me that He too is looking for a replacement. So, I to say to myself, someone has decided not to obey and/or has passed on, left their post and unable to obey so there is a vacant position. God is looking for a replacement.

I clearly know why people use the term King and Queen because we are striving to elevate the mindset which hopefully, will transform the behavior of those who are referred to by this title. I realize that the word says, "speak those things that be not as though they were," and the word is true, but the word Queen and King carry with it responsibility, character, integrity, courage, compassion and dignity. This is a lot to live up to. Do you have what it takes to be Queen? Not to mention the main character of the story, Esther is a Jew and an outsider in a foreign country. Could she really be the next Queen? I'm wondering whether Meghan Markle feels like an outsider in

England? I watched the Royal Wedding knowing that she was not born British or in the royal blood line. She was chosen.

Now finally, I want to address the word anointing. The most famous scripture that is found in Esther is quoted often and located at Esther 4:14, "who knoweth whether thou art come to the kingdom for such a time as this?" I come from an Apostolic/Pentecostal background. When I was younger I thought the anointed/anointing meant someone who could speak in tongues, run around the church, jerk, scream, shout until they fainted and pray for hours at a time. When I got older and was taught, I learned that someone who was anointed was someone who was chosen, prepared, positioned and performed and/or used by God to do specific tasks to upbuild His Kingdom, people and give Him Glory. Sure, the person was connected to, worshipped and had a wonderful relationship with God. But the real test of their "anointing" showed up during the test, trial, pain, processing, problem, trouble and hardships of life. The anointed person's reliance and dependence on God really was known when the person was faced with the lions in the lion's den, beatings, imprisonment and torture that the men and women of God faced. When faced with hardships, God's supernatural power and authority was expressed, descended rested on His anointed people to rescue or deliver his people and show forth His Glory.

Once in a vision God showed me oranges and olives being crushed. He said, "I can't get the juice out of the orange or the oil out of the olive until it is crushed. I can't get the anointing out of you until you are under pressure and crushed. What's in you will come out." I said all of that to say that Esther's anointing, appointment and assignment didn't arrive until trouble and/or a problem arose. The real proof was seen with her agreement with the Will of God, submission to the Plan of God and her willingness to Perform to fulfill her Purpose from God. How do you handle trouble? What happens when you are under a real attack? Haman, the villain, wanted every Jew eliminated not just talk about them, hurt their feelings, damage their reputation or see them just driven out of the Kingdom and/or positions but killed.

Now before you close the book and say, "I'm already married and not looking to marry into the royal family and this book doesn't apply to me." You may be a widow or divorced, young or single reading this and have no desire to be a princess or curious as to how this book applies to you. I'm glad that you thought it and decided to ask.

God's word says in I Peter 2:9 (KJV), "But ye are a chosen generation, a royal priesthood, an holy nation, a peculiar people; that ye should shew forth the praises of him who hath called you out of darkness into his marvellous light." There is a price for this position. There is something that we have to do, change, add, remove and discard from our lives to be the royalty that God is calling and looking for. Are you a Queen? God is looking for a replacement. Let's find out what He is looking for.

What is a Queen

The Book of Esther

 A Queen is defined in Dictionary.com as a "a female sovereign or monarch. the wife or consort of a king. a woman, or something personified as a woman, that is foremost or preeminent in any respect.." When I think of queen I think of rulership, governing, reigning over a country or industry and finally, being the best at or dominant at what is done, i.e. "The Queen of Publishing." That's what they call me. Lol. I digress but it is true. Having the knowledge, ability, fortitude, grit and stamina to rule and actually be a queen at something, is a daunting task and one that shouldn't be taken lightly. Now, one of the biggest mistakes that people and especially women make is comparing their kingdoms, abilities, gifts, talents, territories or opportunities that are placed in their path. Instead of being the "best" or doing the "best" at what is placed in the individual person's hands, they strive to have, be, do and compete with someone else. So, are you striving to be the Queen of your own destiny or someone else's? Are you wanting to dominate and conquer someone else's territory or create your own path by being a maverick or trailblazer? What has God called you to be a Queen over? What does He want you to rule, reign, govern, preside, create and produce in your own

Kingdom or backyard? It is possible for us all to win. It is possible for us all to be Queens. Two people may do the same thing but never will they do it the same way. There is a Queen down inside of all of us waiting to come out and be great. Will you sit back and just criticize others who are making strides with their Kingdom or will you walk out by faith into your own? Where is your Kingdom? What do you dominate? You are the Queen of what...?

Prayer: Lord, make me into the Queen you want me to be. In Jesus' Name. Amen.

_____

_____

_____

_____

_____

_____

_____

_____

_____

_____

_____

_____

_____

_____

The King Needs a Queen

Esther 1:19 - "If it please the king, let there go a royal commandment from him, and let it be written among the laws of the Persians and the Medes, that it be not altered, That Vashti come no more before king Ahasuerus; and let the king give her royal estate unto another that is better than she."

Queen Vashti

 In the beginning of Esther, the King had a banquet that lasted for days. Everyone was drunk, not just intoxicated but drinking for several days makes you drunk. The King decided that he had paraded everything else in his kingdom why not parade his wife, the Queen as well. Her job was to come out, be viewed and entertain the guests by her beauty. Now, I am quite sure that most of us would not have wanted to be around intoxicated people and especially men, but this was a different time and somewhat different perspective toward women. You really didn't get a choice. There are some great things about being queen and not so great things about the job. You have to decide. No one is perfect, not even the queen but it is a powerful position and one that is scrutinized to the highest extent. So, the king and the kingdom need a queen. Are you that lady who is able to perform during the good, bad, ugly and not so fun times or just when it is convenient?

In Esther 1, when Queen Vashti refused to come and be seen during the banquet, the leaders said that a replacement must be found. Why? Because if the queen refused, it would set a standard for other women throughout the kingdom. Her defiance and refusal could destroy the hierarchy, leadership, authority and order of all of the homes and relationships throughout the kingdom. A travesty. Something must be done. A replacement immediately must be found. For the sake of the King's reputation and the state of the Kingdom, there must be a replacement for the Queen.

The King must have a Queen. Who is she? Where is she? What does she look like? Who is best suited for the King? Who will help the Kingdom maintain its honor, dignity and status? Look around your kingdom. No matter if you are married, single, divorced or widowed, you are a queen. The King of Kings needs a Queen. Are you that lady? Is there royalty in your bones whether you have a title or not? The title of Queen doesn't make you a queen. What makes you a queen is what is down on the inside. The King needs a Queen. The Queen is?

Prayer: Lord, who shall be the Queen in the Kingdom? You are preparing your bride. Help me to be that Bride for you. In Jesus' Name. Amen.

Hadassah Means Compassion

Esther 2:7 - And he brought up Hadassah, that is, Esther, his uncle's daughter: for she had neither father nor mother, and the maid was fair and beautiful; whom Mordecai, when her father and mother were dead, took for his own daughter.

 Before she was Queen Esther, her name was Hadassah. Hadassah means compassion. Wow, what a name for a queen. Compassion is defined as "a feeling of deep sympathy and sorrow for another who is stricken by misfortune, accompanied by a strong desire to alleviate the suffering." (https://www.dictionary.com/browse/compassion?s=t) Oh how our world would be such a better place if there were more compassionate people. Now, I confess that compassion is a feeling but also an action word. If you truly feel some type of way about something, a true indicator will be your action and reaction. Hadassah or Queen Esther was compassionate on the inside but that compassion made her do something about the status of the people of God in a strange land bondage. When threatened, Queen Esther was willing to take a risk. She risked her power, her position and her own life to save others. I know people who are willing to risk anything for themselves, their families and certainly not someone else.

Saying, "I feel sorry for someone," is good. But, your compassion turned to action will not only make you feel good but also help do some good in your community, state and our world. The kingdom needs a queen that will have compassion and act for the betterment of others not just themselves. A real queen does what is best for the Kingdom. So, what are you compassionate about? Who have you shown compassion to? What have you done about it lately?

Prayer: Lord help me to have compassion on those that you place in my path. In Jesus' Name. Amen.

_____

_____

_____

_____

_____

_____

_____

_____

_____

_____

_____

_____

_____

_____

_____

It Still Takes a Village

Esther 2:15 - "When the turn came for Esther (the young woman Mordecai had adopted, the daughter of his uncle Abihail) to go to the king, she asked for nothing other than..."

 Hadassah had parents but they were killed. The bible doesn't say exactly what happened to her parents. There could have been war, disease or any number of things that happened seeing as the children of Israel found themselves in captivity. Even though Hadassah's parents were deceased, she was not left without a covering, parents or guidance. Mordecai took her in, adopted her and took care of her. Now some of you reading this may say, I wasn't raised by my parents or I was adopted but know that God placed someone to guide you, give you good advice and try to help you along life's journey. The African proverb, "it takes a village to raise a child," is true. Parenting is a sensitive subject for many because of the dysfunctional and at times, horrific upbringing but whether it was a lady down the street, a teacher, a person at church or a counselor at the boys and girls club, someone has been looking out for you. God makes sure of it. You may not have recognized it at the time and may have brushed it off as a nosey, intrusive person but God may have sent them to you specifically for where you were going, Queen.

Mordecai was that person for Hadassah. He saw something wonderful in her that could benefit many people. He guided, protected and gave her specific instructions throughout the process of being Queen. Look back on your life, who did God send to help you? I had two wonderful parents in my own life who raised me, cared for me and walked with me through all of the major steps of my life. But, they couldn't be everywhere at the same time. There were times they were at work, out of town or I had moved and God brought other people to me that were up close and personal to advise me and help me navigate some very tough times in my life. Like me, you may have had two biological parents but I have a lot more parents, counselors, guides, doors opened, introductions, criticism, instructions given than you can imagine to get me to this stage and place in life. To all of them I say thank you and I appreciate all that you did and said to make me the Queen I am today. Who are your parents?

Prayer: Lord, I thank you for my biological parents, godparents, adopted parents or those that you sent to me when I needed a parent in my life. Bless them for all that they imparted into me on this journey. In Jesus' Name. Amen.

Student for Life

Esther 2:10 - Esther had not revealed her
nationality and family background, because
Mordecai had forbidden her to do so.

 As a teacher, I can recognize a teachable spirit right away. Why? Because the teachable person can normally listen and follow instructions. Secondly, a teachable spirit is calm, removes distractions and wants to get exactly what the teacher/parent/instructor or leader is saying. They don't want to miss anything. They want to have all that they need to be able to complete the task. In Esther's case, she needed all of the instructions of Mordecai, the eunuchs and the assigned handmaidens or anyone else that was seeking to influence her in a positive manner. The instructions were clearly life changing. People's lives were depending on her getting the instructions correct. She had to be a pupil at all cost. A nation's lives were hanging in the balance based on her knowledge, clarity of the instructions and being able to carry them out correctly.

Are you teachable? Do you have to be the smartest, know everything, interrupt when someone else is talking to get your two cents in or are you teachable? There is an old saying that you can learn from anybody. Can you? Some people don't feel like they can learn from someone unless they have more degrees, experience or knowledge about a subject but children have taught me as much as

I've taught them in the classroom. My grandfather was illiterate until he died but I quote things that he said every day of my life. Why? He had wisdom and life smarts even if he was unable to go to school and college. He was teachable and learned when some college educated people still continue to make life mistakes and unable to live the abundant life because they didn't learn the first time. They didn't take to heart someone with more life knowledge than book knowledge.

Be more observant. Learn from others. Open your mind and heart to receive sometime rather than showing off how much you know. Are you a real pupil and willing to learn each day? If not, pray Lord give me a teachable spirit.

Prayer: Lord bless me to always have a teachable, trainable spirit. In Jesus' Name. Amen.

Bring Your Petition to the King

Esther 5:6 - As they were drinking wine, the king again asked Esther, "Now what is your petition? It will be given you. And what is your request? Even up to half the kingdom, it will be granted."

 As children, we would go back and forth between my mother and my father asking them permission to do something. My mother would say, "Did you ask your father." We would then go to my father and he would ask, "What did your mother say." This back and forth between both parents kept unity in the house. My parents wanted to be on one accord with their judgements and commandments to my sisters and me. So, in our house, you had to petition or ask or plead with both the queen and king of the house. In Esther's case, the King had the final say. If the King said, no, that was it and there would be death to children of Israel.

Now as children in our house, we waited until my father had eaten, took a nap and was relaxed before we asked him anything. Why? If he were tired, hungry or busy doing something else, he would probably say no immediately. We learned early to be strategic with our petitions or requests. We knew when it was a bad time or good to ask anything.

Esther was no different. She made sure that she looked good, smelled good and that the King's mood was good before she petitioned him. The rule was that if he didn't extend his scepter to the petitioner that you could be killed. In our house, if daddy said no, it was no. My mother didn't go against my father. If mama said, yes, it was yes and daddy probably wouldn't go against her. How good are you at petitioning, asking or making a request? Do you wait for the right time or do you ask when it is convenient or the right time for you? Do you prepare a perfect setting of food, scenery and atmosphere before you ask?

The same is with the King of Kings. The atmosphere should be set for petitioning. You desire to hear the King say yes and not no. Your petition should be seasoned and wrapped in love, worship and praise. Don't leave out service and humility. The King of Kings has all power. He sits on the throne waiting for you to ask. Don't waste your time with weighty words but come with a humble heart, sweet spirit and atmosphere of worship to transform your petition into permission granted. A yes from the King will change everything. Petition the King! Let's go!

Prayer: Lord grant me the petition according to your plan and will for my life. In Jesus' Name. Amen.

Prayer and Fasting Lifestyle

Esther 4:16 - Go, gather together all the Jews that are present in Shushan, and fast ye for me, and neither eat nor drink three days, night or day: I also and my maidens will fast likewise; and so, will I go in unto the king, which is not according to the law: and if I perish, I perish.

 As a child and now as an adult, I like food. I always have and always will love food. There are some times in life where I don't want to eat. I'm either sick, busy or something is bothering and has me so distracted that I don't eat. The bible tells us that Queen Esther called a fast not only for the children of Israel but for herself and her maiden staff. Now, I don't know if her maidens were Jew or Persian but they did as the Queen commanded. The seriousness of the matter caused them to not only petition but pray and petition Jehovah God of Israel and also "Pass on Food." Fasting is a great cleansing for the body and some people fast from certain foods, water or other staples for health. But, this situation that called for fasting was for more than just to lose 5 pounds or to feel better. This was another life and death situation that Israel found themselves in. It was a job for Jehovah and to show Jehovah how serious, they turned their plates down. Do you have something in your life that is so serious that you are willing to pray, fast, worship, petition and go to war about? There are some things that God specifically brings in your life to see just how serious you are about the source of your relief. Will you go to God in prayer and fast from your food to get your petition answered? Will you just let the problem stay, grow and fester to a much larger problem that could take someone's life, spiritually and literally or are you willing to miss a few meals to see deliverance? Come on Queens! What will it take to see your children, the community and our world changed? This is war! The enemy hates you and wants to see you die not just stopped or to pause but die. Prayer +Fasting +Worship +TheWord = Deliverance. Let's go Queen!

Prayer: Lord, I lay aside everything that will hinder the answers to my prayer including food and/or other distractions that may delay or deny the blessings that you have for me. In Jesus' Name. Amen.

You Are Gifted

Esther 2:7 - Mordecai had a cousin named Hadassah, whom he had brought up because she had neither father nor mother. This young woman, who was also known as Esther, had a lovely figure and was beautiful.

 There was a song at my home church that talked about faith but the phrase used mostly was, "you don't need a lot but use what you got." Now grammatically that might not be correct but Esther used what she had been blessed with for the next position as Queen. Esther was beautiful. She used her beauty to find favor with man and the King. Now some people question utilization of her beauty to gain an advantage. We could be in a discussion for a long time about whether this was right or wrong, moral or immoral, but it worked. There were so many people saved because she was gifted by God with a lovely figure, shape and face. Now her body and face attracted the King but what was in her head and came out of her mouth was so much more than what was on the outside. The Queen possessed wisdom, knowledge, understanding and gifts that kept and held the King's attention until her requests were granted. The old saying, "you catch more bees with honey than with lemons." My thoughts are that when you draw them in, catch them or they catch you, what do you do next? What do you say? How do you answer the questions or phrase the words that will get your message across? That's the real gift that Queen Esther possessed. Her looks got the King's attention but her smarts kept the King's attention and saved a nation.

What is your gift? What talents do you naturally possess? What is in your hands, heart, head or mouth that God wants to use? Have you used it or are you hiding it behind being shy, tired, timid or angry? There are many people that are counting on you whether you know it or not. You Gifted Queen, what's in your hands?

Prayer: Lord, your word declares that my gifts shall make room for me. I surrender all of my gifts for your glory.

Use me as you will. In Jesus' Name. Amen.

Lord, Prepare Me

Esther 2:12 - Now when every maid's turn was come to go in to king Ahasuerus, after that she had been twelve months, according to the manner of the women, (for so were the days of their purifications accomplished, to wit, six months with oil of myrrh, and six months with sweet odours, and with other things for the purifying of the women;)

 The boy and girl scouts' motto is to always be prepared. They teach you all of those life skills about being prepared. What to carry with you in the wilderness, what to carry with you in the woods and do with the equipment if something happens while you are in the wilderness. How to get out of a tough situation and be brought to safety is what being prepared is all about. Preparation is a journey. Preparation is developed over time and you really don't know how prepared you are until you get in the heat of the battle or until you get in a fight.

Girl and boy scouts know how prepared they are when they get in darkness and they need a flashlight or when it starts to rain or they're in a thunderstorm and they have their rain gear they're prepared and have what they need.

It was the same for Esther. She was prepared to be Queen. She may not have known she would one day been Queen until the opportunity was presented to the Kingdom. Mordecai had raised her after her parents were deceased. Mordecai entered Esther into the contest to see who would be the next Queen. He knew she was beautiful but it never mentioned in the bible that Mordecai was assured that Esther would be the next Queen.

How prepared was Esther to take on the role as the next Queen? You really don't know how prepared you are until you're in it. And Mordecai didn't really know either but he took a chance on Esther. He had to have known that she would do well in the King's house or he wouldn't have entered her in the contest.

So how prepared are you queen? Have you been preparing yourself for your next level? Do you have a coach, mentor or person that you are modeling your behavior, business and/or ministry after?

Now, let me get you ready because you don't know how prepared you really are until problems and trouble comes. If trials, trouble and problems have come to you, it's just a test of how prepared you really are. Additionally, more importantly, you have to prepare to win. I find that more people are prepared to fail rather than to succeed. Why? Because there are people everywhere who give you reasons for not trying, not working hard, not going for it or not to do anything. But, what if you win? Prepare yourself for the successful business, ministry and/or career.

Come on, queen. How prepared are you? Let's get prepared to win.

Prayer: Lord, prepare me to be a sanctuary and servant for your purpose and plan. In Jesus' Name. Amen.

_____

_____

_____

_____

_____

_____

_____

_____

_____

_____

_____

_____

_____

_____

_____

Processed to Be Presented

Esther 2:8 So it came to pass, when the king's commandment and his decree was heard, and when many maidens were gathered together unto Shushan the palace, to the custody of Hegai, that Esther was brought also unto the king's house, to the custody of Hegai, keeper of the women.

 Amazingly enough, there's a process for everything. There's a process for food preparation. There's a process that people have to go through to make a car. There's a process for everything. Anything that works well, it has a process. Now we love to say, oh, we eat all-natural foods and everything's organic, but even things that are made outside and not put through a processing system is still through a process. You still have to put the seed in the ground. You still have to put dung around it. Since the seed is in the ground, it is in dirt. It still has to be watered. It still has to be weeded. There's a process for everything. Everything has a process. There's a process to be queen processing to be processed. It's a journey. It's a testament of your endurance. It's a testament for your ability to be put forth your best effort through the process. Pain, hurt, heat, cold, whatever the processing is.

Can you stay in the process to ultimately be Queen? The process is teaching and helping you to sustain and endure. Are you able to endure good times and bad? Are you able to put up with it? Are you able to sustain success or keep it up? Because that next level will require something else that you'd never done or experienced before. Some things you are about to see, you've never seen this before. Why? Because you've never been on this level before. Esther had never been queen or even been a princess. She didn't fully know what was required. Looking in from the outside is not the same as being on the inside and observing from the inside.

For example, some of us don't like paperwork. We give up if there are too many papers, too many forms to fill out and too many people to call and/or the process takes a long time and it is slow. Some of us are unwilling to ask, what is the process for me to be the queen of my life, to be the queen of my career, to be the queen of this situation, to be the queen of my industry and be the queen in my house. There's a process. There are some things I have to do and some things I will need to stop doing. There are some people, places and positions that I have to move away from.

Queen Esther wasn't even allowed to be in Mordecai's house any more. She had to be moved into a special chamber with certain people that she didn't know, and of course remember she was a Jew. She was from the outside, so she was being processed for a position that she wasn't even born for. She wasn't even in line to be the next anything but to be a woman and hopefully, someone's wife. The position wasn't due or owed to her. It was not her rightful inheritance, but God had a reason. So, are you willing to go through the process? Because if you say no, there's somebody else he will choose.

But, know that God picked you. If you say no, if you're unwilling and say that I can't take this process, God's will must be done.

I encourage you to go through the process because you just never know what's on the other side. Stop wanting what someone else has because you don't know what they had to go through to get there. Your process and processing may be totally different than someone else's. Are you ready for the process? You can't get to the next level or position unless you're willing and say yes to the process.

Prayer: Lord help me to go through the process. In Jesus' Name. Amen.

He Chose Me

Esther 2:17 - And the king loved Esther above all the women, and she obtained grace and favour in his sight more than all the virgins; so that he set the royal crown upon her head, and made her queen instead of Vashti.

 So, when I was a child, I wasn't picked for anything sports related. Sports was not my natural gift. I was musical and creative and all those other things. Now it's not to say I didn't have friends and nobody liked me, but I just wasn't athletic. I knew that, but of course the rule in school was everybody had to participate and everybody had to be in the kickball game and everybody had to be in dodge ball and everybody had to try.

When it came to climbing that rope, Lord help me, Jesus, I hated the most. I was not gymnastically gifted. I was not athletic. I couldn't run fast. I could walk. I always dressed out for gym class but I was terrible.

And most of the time when it came to athletics I was picked last. Out of all of that processing and all that preparation was picked by the king. It says that he picked her, he chose her. In chapter two verse 17, not only did he choose her because she smelled good but also because she looked good. She was beautiful. The king loved Esther. She won his heart. He picked her because he loved her above everybody. They brought women to him from all over the kingdom. Can you imagine what that would be like to be picked out of hundreds or thousands? Selected, chosen, handpicked, out of all that you've been through it all, what they told you and all the instructions he picks you, they pick you.

You got the job, you have the position. You are now chosen. Oh, my goodness. Now can you catch your breath? No, you can't catch your breath because you have to live out the responsibility of being selected.

It is now time for you to choose the role, responsibility and title back. Live it, walk it and be to the fullest what you've been selected to do. Know that it comes with obligation. Know, that being picked now takes you up a notch, makes you a target as well, but you were picked. So, we'll worry about all the bad stuff later. We'll worry about all the problems and issues and all the other stuff, but know, you're picked you're chosen. They want you above everybody else. Queen you're chosen.

Prayer: Lord, you have chosen me and I am grateful. Help me to never disappoint you and for you to be pleased with my service.

I'm Favored

Esther 2:17 - Now the king was attracted to
Esther more than to any of the other women,
and she won his favor and approval more than
any of the other virgins.

 I wonder if Mordecai had any
other children and were they
daughters or sons? The
scripture doesn't mention any other
children. So if Esther was the only child
in Mordecai's charge, he had no choice.
What if he had other daughters? How do
you think they would have felt that
Esther was preferred or favored over
them?

There's something about being a favorite
that carries with it a responsibility but
always a knowledge of jealousy from

other people when you're the favorite. When you are the favorite, you always seem to get preferential treatment.

The king had picked Esther already and he picked her above all the other maidens in the Kingdom. Not only did the king's favor her, she was the favorite everywhere. She went from Mordecai's house to the house for the women to the King's palace. She was known in the courts and favored among the eunuchs or guards and/or keeper of the women. Esther was favored by all the servants in the king's palace. Excuse my language but, "favor ain't fair and it sure feels fabulous," is a quote from a gospel song. The life of favoritism is not easy. You have to have what I say, your big girl panties on. You gotta have a strong backbone. You gotta have thick skin to be preferred. You gotta' be able to hear and not hear. You've gotta' be able to see and not see. You gotta' have a bird's eye view. You got to have focus. You got to be driven. You've got to have stamina. You can't get easily distracted. You can't get easily discouraged. You can't get down in the dumps and depressed because people are talking about you because you are preferred because you are favored. You don't have time to sit back and enjoy the favor, but favor has a purpose. You're on a mission. You got something to do. You got something to accomplish. You've got a job to do. You've got a mission to accomplish your purpose, to fulfill your destiny. Queen, you are preferred and favored, now walk in it.

Prayer: Lord I thank you for your favor that you have placed over my life but more importantly give me stamina, courage and wisdom to handle the position and responsibility of favor.

Get in Position

Esther 5:1 - Now it came to pass on the third day, that Esther put on her royal apparel, and stood in the inner court of the king's house, over against the king's house: and the king sat upon his royal throne in the royal house, over against the gate of the house.

 To me, there is nothing worse than being in a position and you can't handle the position or there is nothing worse than you now have a position, but you're still acting as you did in a former position that you had, especially on a job. You're still trying to act like you were in the other position when you're no longer there, especially if you've been promoted.

Queen Esther was in the right position for the king to see her and invite her to the royal house where he sat upon the royal throne. Her petition was requested because she was in the right position, at the right time to be seen by the right person who could answer her request. The king loved her so that he said, "Anything you want Esther up to half of the kingdom is yours."

So, ask yourself, what position are you in? Whether you placed yourself there or there because of other circumstances, are you where God has told you to be? He's been telling you over and over and over again, specific things. Get away from those people. Get out of that church. Get away from that job. Go back to school. You're in the wrong spot. I want you to be here. Yes, it's terrible and it feels uncomfortable and know your Mama didn't raise you that way and nobody else has gone to college, but nobody else desires to be an entrepreneur but you, but you're in the wrong position and God has chosen you and picked you for specific things. You gotta get in the right position for it. You've got to get your placement right where you're supposed to be. You're in the wrong place. The blessings, not there. It's over there. The blessings here, it's over there. Come one Queen, get in the right position.

Prayer: Lord help me to stay in the position that you have ordained and predestined for me to be. In Jesus' Name. Amen.

Performance: The World is Your Stage

Esther 5:2 - And it was so, when the king saw Esther the queen standing in the court, that she obtained favour in his sight: and the king held out to Esther the golden scepter that was in his hand. So, Esther drew near, and touched the top of the scepter.

 I'm a creative arts person. I love all of the creative arts. Whether you're writing, whether you're singing, dancing, whether you're a step thing, whether you're doing spoken word, whether it's ballet, whether it's a music, singing, playing instruments, it doesn't matter. It doesn't matter. I love all of the creative arts and there's nothing better_paying your money to see an excellent performance. People who perform at that top of their game, the best of their ability and can change someone's life if you just perform to your best ability performance. There's nothing worse than jockeying for position. You're striving to be this. I want to be that, but once you get there in that spot, the placement, you won the job, do what you're supposed to be doing. Queen Esther did it through the process, went through the preparation and then performed. When it was time to stand up to the challenge of that position that she found herself in, she performed to the best of her ability. Which in turn 'saved much people alive. Why? Because she performed when it was time to perform. She did it. She actually did it.

So, what are you being asked to perform? What are you being asked to do? Are you studying? Are you watching other people do it? Are you being a student? Do you have a coach? Queen, do you have a mentor? This is the performance of a lifetime. God is the executive director who was determined and made everything ready and prepared just for you. You got the job. The role is yours. Now it's time Queen for you to perform the best performance of your life!

Prayer: Lord help me to perform according to your script and direction for my life. In Jesus' Name. Amen.

_____

_____

_____

_____

_____

_____

_____

_____

_____

_____

_____

_____

_____

_____

_____

You are Protected to Protect

Esther 2:22 - And the thing was known to Mordecai, who told it unto Esther the queen; and Esther certified the king thereof in Mordecai's name.

 So my husband and I have no biological children, but we helped to raise and take care of many other children. Because we have no children, he and I are extremely protective of each other. If somebody says something or does something to either one of us, we are quick to run to the defense and quick to defend because it's just us. Queen Esther was not only protecting herself, she was protecting Mordecai, her family and an entire nation from being destroyed. Being able to protect someone, especially when you're in a position of power is vital and important.

There are people that get into positions of power and forget to protect the people who elected them. For example, the children, the mentally ill, the homeless and the veterans. They forget to put things in place that will provide for those that struggle to provide for themselves.

Queen Esther never forgot who she was, who she represented and what her mission and purpose was for being in that position. There are times that you are protecting people and they don't even realize what you are doing but God sees you. You are in position to protect others and He sees you and will reward you in secret and in the open. Queens can be protection for those who cannot protect themselves. Lord, make me an instrument of protection.

Prayer: Lord, I thank you for your protection and my ability to help protect others from the enemy. In Jesus' Name. Amen.

_____

_____

_____

_____

_____

_____

_____

_____

_____

_____

_____

_____

_____

_____

The Plot Revealed

Esther 2:21 In those days, while Mordecai sat in the king's gate, two of the king's chamberlains, Bigthan and Teresh, of those which kept the door, were wroth, and sought to lay hands on the king Ahasuerus.

Esther 4:7-8

7 And Mordecai told him of all that had happened unto him, and of the sum of the money that Haman had promised to pay to the king's treasuries for the Jews, to destroy them.

8 Also he gave him the copy of the writing of the decree that was given at Shushan to destroy them, to shew it unto Esther, and to declare it unto her, and to charge her that she should go in unto the king, to make supplication unto him, and to make request before him for her people.

Mordecai discovered two plots. The first one was designed to kill the King. Yes, the King. The second plot was supposed to kill the children of Israel. Both plots were evil. When he discovered the plots, he told his authorities. The people were killed who were trying to kill the King but Mordecai was not rewarded for telling. But when Mordecai told the plot to Esther, she did something about it. The scripture tells us to give honor to whom honor is due. The King did just that once it was brought to his attention about the plot. You are not always rewarded for doing your job or the right thing. You have to be okay with somebody else getting the credit, but keep doing good and sooner or later, someone, somewhere will reward you openly.

So what do you do with the plot? When you find out about a plot, do you try to squash it and stop it for the greater good of the kingdom, for the greater good of the project, for the greater good of the church, for the greater good of your family, for the greater good of your company, for the greater good of your life and career or do you just let the plot go on and you turn the other cheek? Are you ready to really be a queen? When you find out about a plot, you gotta make the right decision. Plots are happening all the time with people that are smiling in your face and talking about you behind your back. So, when you find out about a plot, what do you do with it? Stop it in its tracks.

Prayer: Lord help me to be a discerner of the enemies' plots, tell authorities and intercede for the plot to be destroyed.

Timing is Everything

Esther 5:5 - Then the king said, Cause Haman to make haste, that he may do as Esther hath said. So, the king and Haman came to the banquet that Esther had prepared.

 A precision tune-up on a car is a tune-up that is designed to make sure that your car runs to its optimal capacity. The car will run exactly as it was meant to run. All cylinders will be on point, fully powered and ready to go when you accelerate. There will be no hesitation, stall or delays when it is time to go somewhere via the car. For our study, the precision in her every move was life changing and lifesaving. In Esther's case, she had to use precision in her every move she made to stop the plot.

In this case, timing truly is everything. This is just not a cute saying. There is no room for mistakes, second guessing or a 'weak link.' All systems must be on 'go.' A devious plot was not only devised but implemented. It had to be stopped because people's lives were depending on it. Queen Esther had the position, power and plan to stop it and so she did with great precision.

Are you a haphazard planner? Do you do things in excellence, strategy and precision or give it your best shot and hope for the best? There are mistakes that happen, problems that arise and emergencies that occur that may not be foreseen that require adjustments. But, a

Queen must move strategically with the intent to win! A Queen knows that her actions will not only impact her but the 'population' and possibly the world. When you do take action, and you should, be prayerful, mindful of others and seek wise counsel but most important plan your strategy and implement the strategy with precision. Queen, timing is everything...

Prayer: Lord you are a God of timing and precision. Help me to always act, move and do what you say when you say it to carry out your perfect plan with precision. In Jesus' Name. Amen.

Plan Your Work

Esther 4:17 - So Mordecai went his way, and did according to all that Esther had commanded him.

 The saying goes, "if you fail to plan, you plan to fail." Having a good plan is critical. Knowing what should happen next is critical. So, what is your plan of action? What do you plan to do? Esther had plot. She had a problem, she had a position, she had a whole lot going on, but she needed a plan to protect the people of Israel. Being able to plan that out and then trust certain people with her plan. You can't tell everybody your plan because when there is a plot, when there's a plan working against you, you need to determine what people are going to help you get your plan across. Be careful, try the spirits, try their motivation, try and see who they are and what their intentions are. But work your plan. Plan your work, write it down, write the vision, make it plain.

Write out the plan, figure out what the plan of actions should be. What resources, supplies or equipment do you need? What steps do you take first? Who do you trust? What people need to be involved in the plan? What's the end result? What's the goal? How are you going to know whether your plan worked or not? Plan your work. Write the Plan on Paper. Work your plan. You're a queen. To make things happen correctly we need a plan. Come on Queen. Let's plan.

Prayer: Lord, you have the perfect plan. Give me instructions. In Jesus' Name. Amen.

_____

_____

_____

_____

_____

_____

_____

_____

_____

_____

_____

_____

_____

How Do You Handle Power?

Esther 4:5 - Then called Esther for Hatach, one of the king's chamberlains, whom he had appointed to attend upon her, and gave him a commandment to Mordecai, to know what it was, and why it was.

 I like to drive my husband's car rather than mine because it has more power. His car is a six cylinder and mine is a four cylinder. Now I can get from point A to point B in my four-cylinder car, but I just can't get there as fast or as smooth as I can in his. I like driving his car even more because it's got more power. When I apply the accelerator, it moves so much quicker and so much faster.

When Queen Esther became queen by being selected, favored and picked from all the handmaidens who applied for the Queen position by the King, she was given a certain level of power. Of course, in that day, women were merely to have children and run households. In my opinion, she had influence even more than power but it was power just the same.

She had power to command her handmaidens. She had a power to command her assistants, guards and grounds keepers enough to get messages back and forth to Mordecai. The King loved Queen Esther so she could pretty much get anything she wanted from him. She had power or influence with the King to do good and/or power to do evil.

Sometimes you don't know how you will react and what you will do in a certain situation until you have the power and authority to do it. When you are able to speak a thing and it happens, that is a powerful place in life. When you're in a position of power, you have to be careful that you don't misuse that power for evil rather than good. We see it every single day how the misuse of power can affect millions of people. Some people use their power to tear down rather than build up. Others use power to bring on a curse instead of a blessing. What are you doing with your power? There is a level power that is given to every person. The power, abilities and influence has been placed in your hands to enable you to achieve your dreams, visions and goals. Are you using it for good? Not just for your family, not just for your life, not just for your career, but if you're in a leadership position, you have the potential for power and influence across the country, across your community and across the globe.

The power of life and death is in your tongue. What are you doing with your power? Are you sitting on it or are you using it? Queen, you've got the power.

Prayer: Lord give me power and authority and the proper use of them for your glory. In Jesus' Name. Amen.

Who are Your People?

Esther 2:14 In the evening she went, and on the morrow she returned into the second house of the women, to the custody of Shaashgaz, the king's chamberlain, which kept the concubines: she came in unto the king no more, except the king delighted in her, and that she were called by name.

 I know you may want to get all the credit and all the glory for whatever you do, but know that nothing can be done great without other people. I don't care what you seek to accomplish whether its bake one pie or sell pies around the world. Write a book or sell books around the world. If you have a ministry, or a lemonade stand, it's going to require people. It's going to require people to support it, to buy into it and people to spread the word and market it. There will be people who will encourage you, invest in you and build you. Nothing worth doing and worth the world knowing about can remain an island.

It takes people to move anything to the next level. Sometimes it's one person who introduces you to another person who introduces you to the world. God gave me a personality that was outgoing and I'm considered an extrovert. I am friendly even if I don't intend to be because I never know where my blessings are going to come from. I never know who's going to help me move it to the next direction. I don't discriminate against color. I don't discriminate against backgrounds, what you look like or dress like.

I never know who God is going to use to bless me.

I don't know who taught Esther about the importance of people but she understood it. She built relationships throughout her journey to the palace with the guards, eunuchs, servants, handmaidens and others to help her with her plan and quest to help her people.

She called a fast before she went into the King and her handmaidens did the same. She had influence over people. I believe it was not only her position but her spirit that was a great influence. Influence comes from how you talk to people and treat people. God doesn't always tell you that upfront you're going to need this or that person, so treat them nicely.

It's going to take people to open up doors and allow you access and those doors only open because of others. It's going to take people to affirm or refer you. Some people are not going to do business with you or associate with you unless you are affirmed and confirmed by others.

Who are the people in your life? Who has God brought in your life to help you, train you, love you and lead you?

Look for the people. Treat the people, right. Be careful how you entertain strangers because some have entertained angels unaware. The people will bless you, if you bless the people.

Prayer: Lord help to serve your people. In Jesus' Name. Amen.

_____

_____

_____

_____

_____

_____

_____

_____

_____

_____

_____

_____

_____

_____

The Population Matters

Esther 4:8 - He also gave him a copy of the text of the edict for their annihilation, which had been published in Susa, to show to Esther and explain it to her, and he told him to instruct her to go into the king's presence to beg for mercy and plead with him for her people.

Esther 4:13 - Then Mordecai commanded to answer Esther, Think not with thyself that thou shalt escape in the king's house, more than all the Jews.

One of the most famous scriptures in Esther is when Mordecai reminds Esther that she is a Jew just like everybody else and just because you're a queen doesn't necessarily mean that you're going to avoid being killed or destroyed. "Who knows whether you are come to the kingdom for such a time as this?"

Let's talk about the population, the general population. The population are considered by some to be expendable, not necessary to society and can be sacrificed for the greater good.

As a person in a political position, supervisory position and/or other leadership position, there are people who are depending on and will be impacted by your decisions one way or another. It is even more important to consider this if you are in a public service position that can help or hurt the general population of the world. I recently reminded a public official to not forget when he is making decisions that there is a population of parents, children and elderly who are impacted by your decisions and you should consider them.

How do you see your community? Are you concerned? Do you even care? What do you do to help the population? God knows all of the more than 7 billion people in the world and He said that every hair on our head is numbered and he knows everyone by name. God said how you treat the least of my little ones, you've done it even unto me. Handle the population with care, Queen.

Prayer: Lord, enlarge my territory and extend my arms to the community and the world. In Jesus' Name. Amen.

_____

_____

_____

_____

_____

_____

_____

_____

_____

_____

_____

_____

_____

_____

Pressure Produces

Esther 4:4 - When Esther's eunuchs and female attendants came and told her about Mordecai, she was in great distress. She sent clothes for him to put on instead of his sackcloth, but he would not accept them.

 So pressure is applied to certain elements to produce other elements. Diamonds are made from coal after extreme pressure is applied. You get olive oil by crushing olives. You can't get orange juice without crushing the oranges. What happens when you're under pressure? What is retrieved from you when someone or something applies the pressure? When you're under pressure, do you eat more? Do you still care about people when you're under pressure or do you lash out or yell in anger? Do you work well under pressure or do you give up? You don't know what's inside of you until pressure has been applied to you.

It's like an artist on stage. You don't really know how good you are as a singer, until you are onstage with a microphone. When the music starts and you start singing, that's the stage pressure. You don't know how strong you really are until you're tested.

Queen Esther was under extreme pressure in her new role. The pressure of keeping Mordecai, the nation of Israel safe and away from Haaman's power and threat of extinction was a cause of pressure.

Pressure is pleasing a king who you know you found favor with, but you must keep him happy to keep your nation and yourself safe while keeping your position. Everything around you can crumble and be destroyed at any moment.

What do people get when you're under pressure? Do you rise to the occasion? Do you come up with a solution? Do you cry? Curse people out? Do you fight? Do you spit insults? No matter what, pressure is going to come. Prepare yourself for it. Have coping mechanisms in place to handle pressure. Keep people in your life that truly love you and can advise you when pressures arise. You have this great life in front of you. Make the most of it. Be your best self. Under pressure, let the fresh oil of preparation, sweet juice of kindness and pleasant fragrance of prayer come forth even more.

Prayer: Lord give me the strength to handle the pressure of life. In Jesus' Name. Amen.

_____

_____

_____

_____

_____

_____

_____

_____

_____

_____

_____

_____

_____

Made in the USA
Monee, IL
03 April 2024